LIVING IN IDGAF-AFGHANISTAN 2: LIVING THERE AS A PERMANENT RESIDENT

TYLER LAZARUS STUMP
"THE LAZZY"
AKA MISTER. E

ISBN
Fonts by Jess Latham. Thank You.
Printed, Distributed and Bound in the United States of America First Printing
SEPTEMBER 2024
Published by He Who Rebels Against All
Oklahoma City, Oklahoma 73106

Hey, Thanks for getting a copy!
IF you like these, check out my other works
XOXO

LIVING IN IDGAF-AFGHANISTAN 2: LIVING THERE AS A PERMANENT RESIDENT

I'm living in IDGAF-Afghanistan as a permanent resident,

Before America elects (selects) a new president.

I say "selects," not sarcastically or with snark.

But the voters may have no actual voice anymore.

Whoever decides this election won't be the regular people(s)

Not me, Not You, Not the Mexican who is illegally voting.

None of us.

It's all being decided for us.

Treasonously.

After Trump nearly died from being assassinated, the deep state and the deep trouble became even worse.

Kamala was somewhere off stage, being guided by handlers and having her speeches made for her, because she could barely and coherently put any of her own ideas together.

She has no plan,
and the plan to Murder Trump had failed.

The Deep state, nestled much deeper inside the government apparatus was having to change plans on the fly.

And I, as the perpetual fly on the wall, already knew where this thing was headed.

The Deep state is putting us in Deep Shit.

And while everyone now realizes just how full of CRAP the american government is,

Duh Gubbah-ment is really the least of all the problems.

cracks knuckles

It took nearly five years for the average person to realize (and wake up) that they had been the victims of clear (DUAL) bioterrorism… between both the virus and the "vaccine."

Attacked twice.

And they sat there, both times, compliantly, and silently through BOTH.

Nearly 5 years had passed.

FIVE.
FUCKIN.G.
Y E A R S.

looks at my calculator app

That's 1,460 days, and 1461 with the leap year day added.

Over 1,400 days and nights passed,
as people kept dying and passing away….

before the gears finally began to turn.

Americans are S L O W.

Slow, Retarded levels of it.

So yes, The GOVVAmmmment was the problem.

People being incredibly dumb was the truly big issue.

Yew cant fix stew-pid.

Which is why… I'm living in IDGAF-Afghanistan, permanently.

My first report went out on May 15th, 2020.

3 months into this fiasco.

It's also one of if not THE world's first report to accurately demonstrate the truth of what was happening, post Wuhan, Post Washington, Post Warsaw and all the now recorded drama that was still to come, way outside the domain of da Bioweapon.

I knew we were under attack within 3 months.

Americans and everyone else around the world couldn't put it together…. even after THREE years.

Three years of pure evil, government authoritarianism, and the resurgence of rebranded, remixed, retarded communism.

Not even then.

Not even after 100 cloth masks and 98 Pfizers.

It just wasn't clicking.
And people were dying in front of them, with the Virus and then…. the shot.

Hell, they were DYING from the shot and still taking more.

For 3 years.
and then another year.

.... and another.

Five. YEARS.

That's half a decade, babes.

You can't be fucking serious it took americans this long.

But I am.

Dead Serious.

As dead as the millions now dead from this orchestrated, planned, engineered event.

So... **5** years went on by.

That's a whole helluva lot of time.

and Honestly, as glad I was the truth got
out,
In a lot of ways, I felt like I had wasted my
time.

And WASTED so MUCH time trying to get
these retailers, outlets, and the common
people to FUCKINNNNNNG SHUT-UP.

and listen.

that's a massive time expenditure that I didn't plan on giving.

At all.

I certainly didn't plan to be caught up inside a bioterrorist event, but nor did I plan on sacrificing FIVE OF MY YEARS 24/7 devoted SOLELY to it.

I was done.

Not in a burnt out, bitter way.

In a "I have new things to do, immediately" way.

I felt like I was running behind, and it was time to CATCH up.

My humanitarian chapter was over.
This batch of humans were really stupid.

I can't save them and I also have given
(more than) enough to TRY and help them.

They are on their own.

Now, it's not about THEM and trying to get
the truth or a message to any of THEM.

I had fully pulled back, and as the USA
pulled out of Afghanistan,

I pulled in, deeper, to IDGAF-
AFGHANISTAN.

I knew, no matter where I was in the world,
that the world was never going to BE the
same.

The shot (a planned, secondary bioweapon) was going to continue to rewrite the map, for the next six to maybe ten years.

People, everywhere, are just going to drop dead from it.
It's now a game of musical chairs with a mRNA platform that's placing strain on their cardiac tissue.

Among other issues it's doing to cells and tissues.

It literally cannot be helped.

Godspeed to all of them.

Regardless if they believe in God or not.

Their fate is spinning and sealed.

As for me…

For the first time in those five (long) years,

I had other plans… besides writing… publishing… and being caught in the meat grinder of this industry.

I wasn't leaving.
wasn't quitting. wasn't taking a break.
wasn't having a sabbatical. wasn't slowing down.

But I was up to other things, while I did (*and do*) **this.**

I think I realized, for the first time, since I had been trapped in the chaos of all this global, americxan, WORLD history….
that a book wasn't going to matter.

Whatever survives the digital purge and is allowed to be passed as literature wont make a difference, way down the line.

Not on this timeline.

And that's not a fatalistic statement nor is it defeatist.

But thinking you can actualize any kind of real, tangible change defeats the purpose of all of it, anyway.

I'm not writing to convince, dawh-lingz.

I'm writing to preserve.

And I'm proud of how much I have preserved and the magnitude of what

exactly I've recorded.
Which is...
Global Genocide.

But in all the dead and dying,

I still have to live.

And I will go on living until a Nuke drops or someone from the mentioned government agencies finallllly comes to take a swing at me.

Either are now possible.

But I suspect, in the line of reporter suspects with me included, they have bigger problems on their hands than someone who exposed their lies.

They're still lying, and still trying to cover their ass.

While they're engaged in that and the American never-ending drama/story continues (to deteriorate)…

I'm making other plans.

This may be a letdown to people, after 20 something books, who expected some kind of grand touchdown, but I am not going to impose or rally some mass awakening government shutdown.

I'm not the savior of this story.

I've said it before.

I'm the messenger, not the messiah to it.

From the start, as my profile and visibility increased from my works and from my writing (Yay), people expected I was some kind of political mastermind with this HUGE, YUGE TRUMPIAN master plan.

No.

Make no mistake, I will continue to act as an activist and agitate (the hell) out of these bad actors that caused ALLLLL of this,

But there is no way that eye, a gay dude,
can fix, correct, reverse or change all of
this.

Not by myself.

Not singlehandedly.
But on,
the other hand,

I have a list of things (penned with
permanent marker) I want accomplished
regarding all of this,

while I am a resident of IDGAF-
Afghanistan.

Period.

Exclamation POINT!

And what would those things be, you ask.
Question Mark?

Things other than this.

And let me explain why.

puts down the pen

Climate Activist Goons Begin Spray
Painting and Throwing Garbage at the
Mona Lisa.

"SAVE THE ENVIRONMENT!!!"

"GO GREEN!"

-- a triple vaccinated Fatty yells as they spray paint the glass and security comes rushing.

Cameras Flash

In another Scene…

Social Media users argue and scream at each other in all CAPS.

"BIDEN IS A PIECE OF SHIT!!!" -retorts the republican.

"YOU ARE A NAZI, FASCIST, BOOTLICKING SCUM!!" -- replies the liberal.

In the background, someone yells that their pronouns are Xi/Xer/Xim. They add the trangender flag to their bio.

Scene Cuts

In another….

Planes fly above the mainland United States,
Leaving a cute trail of poisonous chemtrails.

"Do you see those????" -- the man from Iowa points out as it flies above them

"See what??" -- the ugly karen replies

"THOSE! those chemtrails…" he responds, flabbergasted.

"Chemtrails" she says, "That's just a conspiracy, Frank."

They both start coughing, five minutes later.

From inside the Whitehouse, Kamala looks into the mirror, trying to memorize her lines before the next CNN interview.

She smoothes her hair and adjusts her blazer as she repeats them back, before she goes out to take questions.

"I will be a president for women everywhere, and I will ensure women can have 97 abortions per quarter. I will be the hope and change this country needs, and the sponsor Pfizer craves. Everyone here will be receiving another booster dose of the covid vaccine, compliments of global genocide, and it's on the house… for anyone who hasn't already died from taking them.

I will be THAT president."

She looks back at the mirror, one final time, pleased with the speech 19 minorities and Haitian migrants wrote for her.

She places an American Flag pin on her shirt, as a finishing touch.

Back in another room in the white house, the current president, Joseph Biden is spilling his Ice cream cone onto his pants, and staring distantly off into the corner.

Jill rushes in and looks disgusted.
--Damnit, this is the third time this week...
"Joe, you're a disgrace," she says, as she storms out.

the Mainstream Media channels all prepare to connect to the Vice president, as another day in a broken America Begins.

scene cuts

images fade

That's why I'm leaving.

and leaving here to do other things.

This circus show won't stop.

It's only going to get worse.

Truly.

And I truly do not give a fuck anymore.

That's why I'm Living in IDGAF-
AFGHANISTAN.

THE END .